SHADOWS OF THE HOLOCAUST
Plays, Readings and Program Resources

By

Harriet Steinhorn

Edith Lowy

cover designed by Madeline Wikler

KAR-BEN COPIES, INC.   ROCKVILLE, MD

"Why study the Holocaust?" students ask, and I answer them thus: Although the victims of this barbaric period were primarily Jews, persecution and human suffering are not limited to a time or to a people. The struggle for human rights continues all over the world, and the lessons of the Holocaust should be learned by every one of us.

I am grateful to Shaare Tefila Congregation of Silver Spring, Maryland and its faculty for their encouragement in writing these plays. I wish also to thank the students who performed them and the parents and children who attended the assemblies. Their warm reception and deep appreciation made my work extremely rewarding. Special thanks are due Clara Gordon, Diane Green, and Naomi Sapir.

—H.S.

The Escape *and* A Precious Gift *first appeared in* World Over Magazine *published by the Board of Jewish Education of Greater New York.*

Library of Congress Cataloging in Publication Data

Steinhorn, Harriet, 1929-
    Shadows of the Holocaust.

    Summary: Five plays about the Holocaust written by a Holocaust survivor.
    1. Holocaust, Jewish (1939-1945)—Juvenile drama. 2. Children's plays, American. [1. Holocaust, Jewish (1939-1945)—Drama. 2. Jews—Drama. 3. World War, 1939-1945—Drama. 4. Plays] I. Lowy, Edith. II. Title.
PS3569.T3792S5   1983   812'.54   83-14887
ISBN 0-930494-25-3

CONTENTS

THE LINE FOR LIFE

In memory of my loving husband,
Irving H. Steinhorn

THE LINE FOR LIFE

A Play in Two Acts

CHARACTERS: TWO NARRATORS
               CAMP INMATES (GABRIEL, JOSHUA, DEBORAH, CLARA, DAVID,
                  ELLEN, HANNAH, HERSHEL, IDA, IRENE, RUTH)
               CAMP COMMANDANT
               TWO NAZI OFFICERS
               OTHER CAMP INMATES
               NAZI GUARDS

TIME: *September, 1942*
SETTING: *The Concentration Camp of Hasag, Verk C, Skarzysko, Poland*

Act I

TIME: *The End of the Day*
SETTING: *Outside the Barrack*
AT RISE: NARRATOR *stands outside the barrack.*

NARRATOR: Hasag, Verk-C in Skarzysko-Kamienna, Poland, was a forced labor camp created by the Nazis at the beginning of the year 1942. Its purpose was to supply cheap, hard labor for the huge ammunition factory complex that was manufacturing war materials 24 hours a day. It also served a second Nazi purpose—to aid in the "final solution" to the Jewish problem. Through hard labor, starvation, mental and physical stress, beatings, and disease, the lives of thousands of young Jewish men and women were cut short.

    As soon as camp inmates became too ill to perform their tasks in the factories, they were taken to a shooting range in the forest outside the camp, where they were killed by the Nazis. The Nazis then turned their guns on healthy camp inmates and forced them to bury the dead. Other young, strong, Jewish men and women were captured in the ghettos all over Poland and brought by trucks and freight trains to replace the dead. At all times, Hasag, Verk C retained 2,000 Jewish inmates who performed only the strenuous, filthy, or dangerous jobs in and around the ammunition factories and farms.

It is Tuesday, September 29, 1942. The last sun rays of the day are forcing their light through the majestic oak and birch trees that cast their shadows on the camp's low, dingy barracks. Some of the inmates have just returned to the camp from various jobs. *(The* INMATES *begin to form a line on stage.)* They are lining up to receive their dinner—a cup of white sugar beet soup and a cup of black coffee substitute. No milk. No sugar. It's the third and last meal of the day.

(NARRATOR *leaves the stage. Two prisoners carry in a big pot of soup and place it on a flat stone in front of the barrack. Men and women continue to form a line.* GABRIEL *and* JOSHUA *are pushing one another and arguing angrily.)*

GABRIEL: Look, I was here first. You are not getting in front of me.

JOSHUA: No you were not! I came before you did, but I had to find Moshe. He has my spoon.

GABRIEL: I don't care what you had to do. The fact remains that you were not here when I got in line, and you are not going to bully me around.

JOSHUA: Ha! Look who's accusing me of being a bully. You're not getting away with it this time. *(JOSHUA and GABRIEL begin struggling with each other.)*

DEBORAH *(Standing in line next to the fighting men):* Shame on you two! Don't we have enough trouble here from the Nazis? Do you have to help the monsters make life even more unbearable? *(JOSHUA and GABRIEL stop fighting and turn angrily to DEBORAH.)*

GABRIEL: I was here first, and this smart aleck is not getting in front of me.

JOSHUA: He was not. I came first, but I left for a minute to pick up my spoon. Moshe doesn't have one, so we share mine.

DEBORAH: Just stop arguing. You are wasting your energy.

GABRIEL *(Holding his stomach):* I'm too hungry to give up my place. My stomach hurts too much. I can't wait a second longer than I have to for my supper.

JOSHUA: Supper? You call that watery mess supper? You'll be lucky if you find three chunks of beets in it.

DEBORAH: Come on, guys, you're acting like children and not like grown men. *(A prisoner runs in and hands the inmates guarding the pot of soup a ladle. One inmate begins to ladle a cup for each prisoner. The line moves.)*

GABRIEL *(Raising his cup to receive his meal and speaking to the inmate who is serving)*: Please, Hershel. Stir up that soup. Have mercy. I will die tonight if I get only water again.
(HERSHEL looks at GABRIEL, mixes the soup, and pours it out. Some of the inmates, including GABRIEL, devour their food as soon as they receive it. The women carry their food back to the barrack. Without a word, they sit down on their bunks and eat the soup. The door opens. DAVID enters the room, hopping on one foot and supporting himself on a long stick.)

DAVID *(Excitedly)*: Hannah! Hannah! I have wonderful news! *(All the girls turn toward DAVID in surprise. HANNAH rises slowly.)* Hannah! You won't believe the wonderful news I heard! You just won't believe it!

DEBORAH: The war is over. Right, David?

HANNAH: What is it? I've never seen you so happy.

DAVID *(Turning to DEBORAH)*: No, the war is not over, at least not yet. Maybe soon. But what would be the next best thing?

IDA: We are going home!

DAVID: *(Now looking sadly at the girls)*: Well, yes and no.

ELLEN: What do you mean, yes and no? What kind of joke is that?

DAVID: It's not a joke.

IRENE: Look, David, we are too tired to play games. It was a hard day.

RUTH: I don't have any strength left to take my shoes off before I go to sleep.

HANNAH: Come on, David, what is it?

DAVID: Okay, this is what I heard. Tomorrow the Nazis will announce that all children under 16 years of age, and all adults over 35 years of age, will be allowed to go home to the ghetto. All the people who are sick and unable to work will be sent home, also. *(The girls look at* DAVID *in disbelief.)*

CLARA: Well, that doesn't qualify many in our barrack. Only Hannah.

IDA: I don't believe it anyway. Why should the Nazis suddenly be so goodhearted?

DAVID: I don't know what the order means. And I'm sorry that all of you can't go home.

ELLEN: But if the Nazis are giving you permission to leave, maybe soon they'll let us go, too.

IDA: How I wish I could believe that.

HANNAH *(Getting excited):* I can't believe it! I just can't believe it! I may be going home! I'll see my father, Rita, Eva!

IRENE *(Placing her hand on* HANNAH'S *shoulder):* Hannah, don't get your hopes up too high. You may be disappointed. The Nazis could change their minds. It wouldn't be the first time.

DEBORAH: It may be just a false rumor.

DAVID: No, I'm sure it's not. But we should know for sure tomorrow.

HANNAH: David, will you be able to walk all the way to the ghetto on your bad leg?

DAVID: Oh, I'm positive I will. I think I could fly home, if the Nazis let me. But maybe the Nazis will put us on trucks. After all, it's about seven miles to the ghetto, and some of the people are sick.

HANNAH: Are you sure you're not dreaming this whole thing?

DAVID: No, I'm not dreaming. I'm happy we'll be going home tomorrow. I wish all our friends were coming with us.

IRENE: Who could ever predict that a time would come when we would actually pray to be in the ghetto again!

ELLEN: We know now that life can be much more unbearable than the ghetto.

IDA: At least we were together with our families.

RUTH: David, it's getting dark. No one here has a watch, but it must be close to 7 o'clock. You'd better go. You don't want to be caught after the curfew begins.

DAVID: You're right. It would be awful to be killed the night before I'm allowed to return home. So long, everyone. (DAVID *leaves.* HANNAH *paces the floor.)*

CLARA: Go to sleep, Hannah. Tomorrow you still may have to go to work.

HANNAH: Oh, I'm too excited. Don't you understand? Tomorrow I may see my father, my sisters, my friends. Oh, I wish that my mother were going home, too.

IDA: If the Nazis are letting people go home from this camp, then maybe the same rule will apply to other camps as well. Your mom may be going home, too.

HANNAH: But she isn't 35 years old yet.

ELLEN: Are you sure? My mother is much older than that.

HANNAH: Yes, I'm sure. It's easy for me to remember, because my mother is exactly 20 years older than I am. I'm 13, so she is 33. *(*HANNAH *goes to her bunk and lies down.)*

ELLEN *(Wistfully)*: How I wish I were going home tomorrow.

RUTH *(Whispering)*: Ellen, think how hurt Hannah will be if it turns out that this is one of those false rumors we have heard so many times before.

ELLEN: But just as many turned out to be true. Somehow I have a feeling that this one is real.

IRENE: Come on, girls, let's get some sleep. I was up all last night coughing. If I don't get some rest tonight, I won't be able to get up for roll call tomorrow. *(Lights go out. The girls lie down. No one speaks.* HANNAH *is twisting and turning.)*

ELLEN *(Sitting up)*: Hey, that gives me an idea! *(Dim lights return to stage.)*

DEBORAH *(Impatiently)*: What now?

ELLEN: Irene, you've been coughing and not feeling well. The Nazis may give you permission to go home.

RUTH: Don't be so naive.

IDA: Anyone trying to survive on the food in this place for more than a week is not well. And many have been here for months.

DEBORAH: Actually, we are probably the healthiest and strongest of all, because we work in the vegetable gardens.

IDA: And our suntanned faces are certainly a contrast to those sickly-looking inmates who slave in the ammunition factories 10 and 12 hours a day.

HANNAH: They look like ghosts whose faces and hair have been colored with yellow paint.

ELLEN: If those gases are powerful enough to turn their skin yellow, just imagine what must be happening to their lungs.

DEBORAH: It's cold-blooded murder to expose humans to these deadly gases without the protection of special gas masks and uniforms.

12

RUTH: And with so little food.

CLARA: That's right. You can't eat bullets, gunpowder, or mustard gas.

DEBORAH: But when the overseer isn't looking, we can steal a carrot, a turnip, or sometimes a cabbage leaf.

RUTH: Just make sure you don't get caught.

IRENE: But if the war doesn't end soon, and we are not freed within the next couple of weeks, we may look just like the workers in the gas factories.

CLARA: Our work in the fields will be ending.

RUTH: Almost all the crops have been harvested.

ELLEN: At the first snowfall, out to the factories we go.

DEBORAH: Please girls, let's just take one day at a time.

IRENE: Then let's stop the chatting and go to sleep. Tomorrow is another back-breaking day.

ELLEN: Hannah, I do hope you will go home tomorrow as David said.

IDA: Oh, please, God, please. We want so much to go home.

CURTAIN

Act II

TIME: *Early morning of the next day*
SETTING: *Outside the barracks*
AT RISE: NARRATOR *on stage; prisoners begin to assemble for roll call*

NARRATOR: Hannah had a terribly restless night. She was too excited to sleep. Her anticipation of returning home was mixed with the fear that the rumor might be false. When she finally fell asleep, Hannah had terrible nightmares. In these frightening dreams she was chased by the Nazis and their hound dogs. She was terror-stricken when they captured her and chained her to the barrack.

When Hannah woke up, she was relieved that her arms and legs could move freely. There was still hope of going home. David was so convincing. She really believed him. Hannah prayed that her mother would be released and would return home, also. In her fantasy, she could see the reunion with her father, mother, and sisters. She couldn't wait to see them all! Hannah's longing for her family and home was so strong that it hurt. Other prisoners, also believing they would be released by the Nazis, couldn't wait for the night to end.

It's morning now. The inmates are lining up for roll call, as they do every morning before work. They are tense and full of expectation. So far there is no indication that this day will be different from any other. (NARRATOR *leaves the stage. Armed* NAZI GUARDS *surround the prisoners.)*

DEBORAH: Where's Hannah? Have you seen her?

ELLEN: No, I haven't.

RUTH: I think she's saying good-bye to friends from the Radom Barrack.

IDA: Hannah is convinced that she is going home today.

CLARA: I do hope she is right.

IRENE: Have you heard anything more?

DEBORAH: No, not a word.

RUTH: But today we've been waiting here longer than usual for roll call.

ELLEN: That may be a good sign.

(HANNAH *joins her friends in the line, taking her place between* ELLEN *and* DEBORAH. *Other friends move to* DEBORAH'S *left.)*

HANNAH: Any more news about going home?

ELLEN *(Sadly):* No, nothing else, but it's still early.

(Two NAZI OFFICERS *enter.)*

FIRST NAZI OFFICER: Achtung! Attention!

SECOND NAZI OFFICER: Those of you who are under the age of 16 or over 35 will be going home today to the ghetto. Some of you who are sick will be sent home, also.

FIRST NAZI OFFICER: The Camp Commandant will be here soon to tell you who leaves and who stays.

(The OFFICERS *move to the rear of the stage.* HANNAH *jumps up joyfully. She hugs* DEBORAH *and* ELLEN. DAVID, *standing farther down the line, waves happily in* HANNAH's *direction. Other inmates hug and kiss one another.* HANNAH *moves towards her friends to say good-bye.)*

ELLEN: Hannah, will you promise to visit my parents and tell them not to worry about me?

HANNAH: Of course. I can't wait to visit them again. I've missed playing with your sister Janie. I wish you were going home to see them yourself.

ELLEN *(Sadly):* I know. So do I.

IRENE: Do you think you could stop by my house, too?

HANNAH: Sure I will.

IRENE: My little brother has been sick for some time. It would make him happy to hear about me. Just don't tell him anything that would upset him.

HANNAH: I'll miss you. You've become my second family. I don't think I could have managed here without your help.

DEBORAH: You managed fine. I'm proud of you.

15

HANNAH *(Hugging* DEBORAH*):* Thank you, Deborah. You set a good example. *(Turning to* CLARA*):* You'll take good care of yourself, won't you?

CLARA: Of course I will. I won't give these murderers any satisfaction. I will live to see them hang!

DEBORAH: That's the spirit, Clara.

IDA: Hannah, you make sure to tell our families that in spite of all the difficulties, our spirits are high.

HANNAH: I will. I do hope all of you will be coming home soon.

IRENE: How I wish I could go with you. Two months and eight days in this living hell is more than enough for any human being.

DEBORAH: No one expected Hannah, David, and the others to be going home, but you see, they are. Who knows? Tomorrow may be our turn.

*(*CAMP COMMANDANT *and the two* NAZI OFFICERS *carrying whips and guns enter the stage.)*

FIRST NAZI OFFICER: Achtung! Attention!

(Silence and fear dominate the stage. The disdain for the camp inmates is visible on the arrogant faces of the well-groomed Nazis. The selection begins. Without a word, the CAMP COMMANDANT *points a finger at a weak or sickly-looking prisoner. The* FIRST NAZI OFFICER *directs the selected prisoners to a separate line.)*

IRENE: Look at these beasts. They think they are gods.

DEBORAH: A nod of a criminal's finger and you are free to go home or to rot in this hell.

ELLEN: I just can't believe it! Are we really living in the 20th century?

IRENE: I feel an urge to scream at the top of my voice what I think of them.

DEBORAH: But you can't. That would be suicide.

IRENE: I want to go home. You want to go home. What right do they have to keep us here?

CLARA: They have no right. But they have the guns and the armies of guards to keep us in.

HANNAH (*Clutching* DEBORAH's *hand):* I'm scared. I'm so scared.

DEBORAH: Don't be. In a few hours you'll be home with your family.

ELLEN: Think of all the joy and happiness that awaits you in just a little while.

RUTH: And all this torture behind you.

IDA: Home with your dad, your sisters, and perhaps your mom, too.

(DAVID *is directed by the pointing finger of the* FIRST NAZI OFFICER *to join the new line. Beaming with happiness,* DAVID *waves his hand toward* HANNAH, *as the Nazis move on.)*

HANNAH: Oh, look. David has been selected.

IDA: Hush. They are coming.

(All *is quiet. Only the click of the Nazi's boots is heard. The* CAMP COMMANDANT *and the two* OFFICERS *are now looking over* HANNAH *and her friends. They pass by without selecting any of them.* HANNAH, *terrified of speaking up to the Nazis and just as fearful of losing her opportunity to return home, musters up her courage as the* SECOND NAZI OFFICER *walks by.)*

HANNAH: Sir, Herr Commandant. I am only 13 years old. Please, I want to go home.

SECOND NAZI OFFICER (*Turning to* HANNAH): You are big and strong. You can work.

HANNAH: But I am only 13. Please, please let me go home.

SECOND NAZI OFFICER *(Pointing his whip at* HANNAH *and very angry):* You go to work!

(The OFFICER *follows the* CAMP COMMANDANT *who selects another prisoner to join those returning to the Ghetto.* HANNAH *is crushed and in shock. Tears flow down her face as she cries quietly. She is unable to utter a sound. Her fists are tightly pressed toward her face. Her head droops, as she sinks to the ground. Her friends comfort her.)*

DEBORAH *(Her hand on* HANNAH'S *shoulder):* I am sorry, Hannah. I am so sorry.

ELLEN: I know how much you counted on going home today.

HANNAH *(Sobbing):* I don't understand. I don't understand.

CLARA: I don't understand either. They said everyone under the age of 16 could go to the ghetto.

FIRST NAZI OFFICER *(Facing the prisoners):* Forward, march!

*(*DEBORAH *and* ELLEN *urge* HANNAH *to get up, as their other friends look on helplessly.)*

ELLEN: We must leave now, Hannah. We must go to work.

DEBORAH: Please get up, Hannah. You will get hurt.

FIRST NAZI OFFICER *(Poking at* HANNAH *with his gun):* Get up! *(*HANNAH *doesn't move.)*

SECOND NAZI OFFICER *(Pushing* HANNAH'S *friends with his rifle):* You are an hour late for work already. Hurry up! Move on!

*(*DEBORAH *and* ELLEN *seize* HANNAH *by the arms and pull her up as the rifle blows fall on them as well. The girls, holding on to* HANNAH, *join the line of workers, surrounded by armed guards. The inmates, sad, hungry, and drained emotionally by the ordeal, walk off the stage. The prisoners who have been selected to go home leave the stage in the opposite direction.)*

18

FIRST NARRATOR: Armed Nazi guards escorted the selected camp inmates to the ghetto. Those prisoners who were too weak or too ill to walk were shot in cold blood. David, though limping and in a great deal of pain from the bad leg infection, did reach the Skarzysko ghetto and was joyfully reunited with his family.

Hannah's father and her two younger sisters visited with David. They learned as much as David would tell them about Hannah and the conditions of Hasag Verk C. The following day, many of the sick and weak prisoners from two other concentration camps located outside the city, Hasag Verk A and Hasag Verk B, also reached the ghetto. The Jewish community welcomed the new arrivals into their badly overcrowded quarters. They shared with them what little was still in their possession.

But their stay in the ghetto did not last long. On October 1, 1942, two days after David arrived home, the Nazis ordered all ghetto residents to assemble in a large courtyard. Jewish leaders were informed that the plan was to resettle the community in Eastern Poland. Each resident was permitted to take a suitcase or knapsack of his belongings for the journey.

All the Jews of the Skarzysko ghetto, including the new camp arrivals, were marched to the railroad station, surrounded by armed Nazi guards. A small group of strong men, including David's older brother, was separated from the group and sent to a labor camp. The rest of the ghetto residents were forced to board freight trains which transported them to their unknown destination. These innocent men, women, and children, including David and his family, Hannah's father and her sisters, all perished in the gas chambers of the death camp of Treblinka.

SECOND NARRATOR: The girls in Hasag Verk C continued their struggle to stay alive against tremendous obstacles—starvation, disease, Nazi beatings and torture, bullets, and gas chambers. Three years and four concentration camps later, Deborah was still alive when British soldiers liberated Bergen-Belsen extermination camp in Germany. She died two days later from starvation and typhoid fever. Freedom did not arrive in time to save her life.

Of the people you have met, Hannah, her mother, Ruth, and David's brother were the sole survivors.

CURTAIN

PRODUCTION NOTES

THE LINE FOR LIFE

CHARACTERS: 7 male; 7 female; 2 Narrators; male and female extras for camp inmates; male extras for Nazi guards.

PLAYING TIME: 20 minutes.

PROPERTIES: A large stone; a big pot or bucket; a soup ladle; cups; spoons; long benches; guns and/or whips.

SETTING: A forced labor camp in Poland, September 1942. Outside the barracks, there is a backdrop of trees, other barracks, and watchtowers. There is a large stone at center stage. Inside the barracks, there are rows of benches and/or a backdrop of the 3-tiered shelves that serve as beds.

COSTUMES: Camp inmates wear shabby clothing. Nazis wear army uniforms with hats or helmets and boots. Red armbands with black swastikas on white circles are worn on their left arms.

LIGHTING: Bright lights during most of the play. Lights are dimmed when the camp inmates attempt to sleep, as indicated in the text.

SOUND EFFECTS: None.

WILL WE BE FREE?

*To my granddaughter, Lena, and to all
my students, our hope for the future.*

WILL WE BE FREE?

A One-Act Play

CHARACTERS: NARRATOR
EVA, DAVID, GITTEL, JOSEPH, LIDA, JUDITH, MOSHE,
RACHEL, RUBEN

TIME: *June, 1942*
SETTING: *An alley in Skarzysko*Ghetto, Poland*
AT RISE: NARRATOR *is center stage. Children are playing.* JOSEPH *is bouncing a ball and playing catch with* MOSHE. *Other children are hopping or skipping. Two or three children sit on the steps talking.* LIDA *sings a lullaby to an imaginary doll.*

MOSHE: Careful with that ball, Joseph. It's the last one we have.

JOSEPH: I know, I know. I am watching it.

GITTEL: It frightens me when I think that this ball will wear out, and soon we won't be playing ball anymore.

RUBEN: We will play imaginary ball, just like Lida is playing imaginary dolls. *(He points to* LIDA.*)*

EVA *(Turning to* ROSALIE*)*: When the war is over, what's the first thing you want your mom to buy for you?

(The boys and girls stop playing and listen to the conversation.)

ROSALIE: I want the most beautiful doll in the world. She will have long hair with a pink ribbon in it...big, blue eyes and rosy cheeks. She will have a purple, shiny dress and shoes to match. She will have...

LIDA: Then she will look just like you!

ROSALIE: Oh no! Not like me. Her hair will be brown, not red. And she will be beautiful!

*pronounced Skăr-zĭs-kō

23

MOSHE: Boy, oh boy, what crazy talk! A baby doll...how can you even think of a baby doll? Aren't you hungry? Doesn't your stomach want to burst from pain?

JOSEPH: Sometimes I am so hungry, I can't even sleep at night.

RUBEN: Gee, would I love to have a roll with butter and lots of cheese!

RACHEL: When the war is over, the first thing I want is scrambled eggs, with bread and lots of butter.

LIDA: I don't remember the taste of eggs anymore.

JUDITH: It's been a long time since I had any.

MOSHE: When the war is over, I will get the biggest chocolate cake you ever saw, and all the milk I want to drink! Glass, after glass, after glass.

EVA: Chocolate cake? What does it taste like?

MOSHE: Dummy, don't you know what chocolate cake is? Didn't you ever have any?

GITTEL: Don't be nasty, Moshe! Eva is too young to remember.

RUBEN: Boy, will she have a lot to learn when the war is over!

(DAVID *comes running, all excited and out of breath.*)

DAVID: Am I glad that my birthday is next week!

(*The children turn toward* DAVID.)

RACHEL: Why? What's so wonderful about it?

JOSEPH: You don't think the war will be over by then, do you?

RUBEN: What good is a birthday party without a birthday cake?

ROSALIE: And no presents!

DAVID: No, no, it's not that! Next week I will be 11 years old. That's all.

CHILDREN: Big deal! *(They turn away from* DAVID.*)*

DAVID: Wait a minute! It is a big deal!

CHILDREN: Oh? Why?

DAVID: A visitor was in our house. I overheard him talking with my parents. *(*DAVID *hesitates and looks around.)* He said that all the children under the age of 10 will be killed by the Nazis.

CHILDREN *(In disbelief)*: You're crazy! That's a lie!

DAVID: No, no, I'm not lying. Honest! I heard him say it clearly. The Nazis will kill all the children up to age 10.

GITTEL: I don't believe it!

(The children are stunned. EVA *is crying.* LIDA *puts her arm around* EVA.*)*

LIDA: Don't cry, Eva. That's not true. God would not permit it! And besides, didn't you hear Mom and Dad talk last night? They said the war will end soon, very soon.

ROSALIE: You will see. Before you know it, we will be back in our homes, away from this dreadful place.

RACHEL: Just think, we will go to school, and have all the books we want to read!

JUDITH: We will have dolls and toys. And all the food we want to eat!

ROSALIE: We will have games and new clothes!

EVA *(Wiping her eyes)*: And birthday parties?

DAVID: Yes, and we will play in the park and forest, just like we used to!

RUBEN: We will swim in the river and build sand castles on the beach!

MOSHE: We will visit our grandparents and aunts and uncles who live in Lodz and other cities!

JOSEPH: We will go to the movies! If only the war would end. Please, God, let the war be over soon!

LIDA: You will see, soon we will be free!

DAVID: Free, like the birds in the sky!

CHILDREN: Like the birds in the sky! *(Imitating flying birds.)*

RACHEL: Free like the buzzing bees! *(Imitating bees.)*

MOSHE: Free like the wind in the trees! *(Imitating the wind.)*

CHILDREN: You will see, we will be free! *(Children walk off the stage.)*

NARRATOR: David did celebrate his eleventh birthday in the ghetto. Although there was no birthday cake, his parents and two sisters tried to make the day very special for him. But three months after David's birthday, in October 1942, all the Jewish children, their parents and their relatives—2,000 Jewish people carrying their few belongings in knapsacks and suitcases—were taken to the train station. They were forced by armed Nazi guards into cattle car trains, and transported to the death camp of Treblinka. There the Jewish community of Skarzysko disappeared forever!

CURTAIN

PRODUCTION NOTES

WILL WE BE FREE?

CHARACTERS: 5 female; 4 male, Narrator.

PLAYING TIME: 10 minutes.

COSTUMES: Shabby children's clothing, sandals or shoes (not sneakers).

PROPERTIES: A child's ball, a dishtowel tied in a fashion to represent a child's doll.

SETTING: Backdrop depicts a ghetto courtyard of houses and buildings.

LIGHTING: No special effects.

SOUND: Lida sings lullaby such as *Raisins and Almonds* or *Tumbalalaika;* children may sing song such as *Am Yisrael Chai* as they exit the stage at the end of the play.

SHADOWS OF THE HOLOCAUST— NOW AND THEN

To Pauline, Ted, Allan, Wendy and Mark, who sustained me with the love, joy, and purpose they brought into my life.

ČESKOSLOVENSKÁ REPUBLIKA

Obvodní   NÁRODNÍ VÝBOR v   Praze 1

OKRES   Praha

RODNÝ LIST

Rady židovských náboženských obcí

V RODNÉ MATRICE ~~XXXXXXXXXXXXXXXXXX~~

v   Praze

VE SVAZKU Fryštát ROC. 1928 NA STRANE 167/8 POD CIS. RADOVYM 1170
JEST ZAPSÁNO

Den, měsíc a rok narození	22.12.1928 Dvacátéhodruhého prosince jeden tisíc devět set dvacetoasm
Místo narození	Orlová-Lazy čp. 263, o. Karviná
Jméno a příjmení dítěte	Edita P i c k o v á
Pohlaví	ženské
Státní občanství	.-.
Jména a příjmení, den, měsíc, rok, místo narození, povolání a bydliště otce, jména a příjmení jeho rodičů	Rudolf P i c k, narozený dne 5.února 1896 v Javorníku, o.Veselí n.Mor., obchodník, rodiče: Samuel Pick Sali roz.Kohnová
Jména a příjmení, den, měsíc, rok, místo narození, povolání a bydliště matky, jména a příjmení jejich rodičů	Irem P i c k o v á, roz.Kornfeldová, narozená dne 1o.srpna 1902 v Porubě, rodiče: Adolf Kornfeld, Franc roz-Freundlichová
Poznámky	.-.

Praze   dne 22.2.1953.

Předseda
V Z.

matrikář.

SHADOWS OF THE HOLOCAUST–NOW AND THEN

A Two-Act Play

CHARACTERS:

ACT I: ALAN, BENJAMIN, DAN, DAVID, ELLEN, JEFF, MARK, REBEKAH, RUTH, SUSAN, MRS. SOLOMON

ACT II: MR. GOLDBERG, MRS. GOLDBERG, JOSEPH, MIRIAM, A NAZI COMMANDER, NAZI SOLDIERS, GHETTO JEWS—MEN, WOMEN AND CHILDREN (SIZE OF THIS GROUP DEPENDS ON STAGE AND CLASS SIZE).

TIME: ACT I — *The present*
           ACT II — *1941*

SETTING: ACT I — *Silver Spring, MD*
           ACT II — *Plock,*Poland*

Act 1

TIME: *The end of a school day.*

SETTING: *Outside a school in Silver Spring, MD*

AT RISE: *The school bell is ringing. Boys and girls (carrying books under their arms) run onto the stage, chatting and calling to each other. They form small groups to wait for their school buses and carpools. Another group of students, their faces serious and somber, quietly enter the stage, joining the other students.* MARK *enters and* DAVID *runs toward him.*

DAVID: Gee, I thought the bell would never ring. Mark, what time will your dad pick us up after dinner tonight?

MARK *(Stunned and confused):* Pick us up?

ALAN: What's the matter, Mark? Did you forget already? *(MARK looks up at the boys but remains quiet.)*

DAVID: The game tonight.

JEFF: At the Capital Centre. Don't you remember?

*pronounced Plŏtzk

31

MARK *(Unenthusiastically):* Oh, that.

ALAN: Hey man, what got into you?

DAVID: Did you get into a fight today?

MARK: No, I didn't get into a fight.

ALAN: Did you flunk the math test?

MARK: No! The test was easy.

JEFF: Are you O.K.?

MARK: I'm fine, guys. Honest, I'm O.K.

DAVID: Then what's on your mind? It's not like you to forget the biggest basketball game of the year.

MARK: O.K. you guys, stop the shouting. *(All the boys become quiet and look up at Mark.)* Today in class we talked about the Holocaust, and I can't get some things off my mind.

DAN: Like what?

MARK: For one thing, how could the whole world stand by and do nothing, not one thing, to prevent the Nazis from murdering six million Jewish people— innocent men, women and little children. How could they?

(The sound of a car horn is heard in the background. SUSAN *runs toward* JEFF.*)*

SUSAN: Come on, Jeff, it's our carpool!

SUSAN *and* JEFF: So long, see you tomorrow!

STUDENTS: See you.

(SUSAN and JEFF leave the stage. The other girls and boys move forward and join ALAN, DAVID and MARK. Some of them sit down on the floor. The curtain falls behind them.)

RUTH: Are you talking about the Holocaust?

MARK: Yes, the Holocaust. Just think, if the State of Israel had existed during World War II, the Nazis would never have succeeded.

REBEKAH: But at that time, the Nazis had the most powerful armies in the world.

DAN: That's right. They armed themselves and prepared for war for many years.

REBEKAH: But you know how long it took the Allies to defeat the Nazis.

MARK: Just the same. Many innocent people might not have been slaughtered, because Israel would have found a way to save them.

ALAN: You mean like what Israel did when they freed the hostages at Entebbe?

MARK: Exactly! Just like Entebbe!

REBEKAH: Why didn't the Jewish people of Europe save themselves?

MARK: What do you mean?

REBEKAH: Well, for one thing, the Jews didn't look any different from their non-Jewish neighbors. So when the Nazis ordered them to move to the ghettos, why did they obey that order?

ELLEN: That's right! Why didn't they remain in their homes?

BENJAMIN: They couldn't force me to leave my home and move to a ghetto.

RUTH: After all, the Nazis were German soldiers who invaded foreign countries. How could these strangers tell who was Jewish and who was not?

DAVID: I guess for us here in the United States, that's difficult to understand.

ALAN: Today in class, Mrs. Solomon explained that question with two birth certificates.

BENJAMIN: What do birth certificates have to do with it?

(MRS. SOLOMON *walks onto the stage, carrying a briefcase.*)

ALAN: Everything. Oh, here comes Mrs. Solomon, maybe she can show you what I mean. (ALAN *walks up to the teacher.*) Mrs. Solomon, would you show my friends the birth certificates we saw in class?

MRS. SOLOMON: Sure, Alan. *(She opens her briefcase.)*

BENJAMIN: I don't understand what a birth certificate will prove.

MRS. SOLOMON: Let me show you. First, let's look at this one.

(She displays a birth certificate from the U.S.A. At this point the birth certificate may be projected on the wall for all to see.)

MRS. SOLOMON: This American birth certificate records your name, your parents' names, and the place and date of your birth.

BENJAMIN *(Impatiently):* I know that. I looked at my brother's just the other day, when he applied for his driver's permit.

MRS. SOLOMON: That's right. All of you have one just like it. But here is a birth certificate issued in Czechoslovakia before World War II.

(As she displays the second certificate, it is projected on the wall.)

RUTH: Is it different from ours? I can't read it.

MRS. SOLOMON: It's exactly the same, with one exception.

STUDENTS: What's that?

34

MRS. SOLOMON (*Pointing to the words*): These Czech words mean that the person is a member of the Jewish religion.

BENJAMIN: What's the connection? I still don't get it.

MARK (*Turning to* BENJAMIN): Don't you see? Every city, town, and village had recorded in their official documents not only the names and addresses of all their citizens, but their religion as well.

MRS. SOLOMON: That's right, Mark. So, when the Nazis invaded these countries, they were able to locate almost every Jewish man, woman, and child.

BENJAMIN: Then why didn't the Jewish people move to other cities or towns where there would be no record of them?

MRS. SOLOMON: They couldn't, Benjamin.

STUDENTS: Why not?

MRS. SOLOMON: One of the very first orders issued by the Nazis prohibited the Jews from traveling. Jews weren't allowed to move to other towns or even go for a visit. Later they were forced to live in ghettos.

DAN: Just because the Nazis gave the orders didn't mean that everybody had to follow them, did it?

MRS. SOLOMON: Some Jews felt the way you do. They disobeyed the orders.

DAN: Good!

MRS. SOLOMON: But most of them were caught and tortured, as a warning to others not to disobey.

RUTH: How were they caught?

MRS. SOLOMON: Nazi soldiers searched the streets outside the ghettos. They inspected trolley cars and trains. They demanded identification. Those who couldn't prove that they were not Jewish were tortured and beaten until they confessed. Sometimes mistakes were made, and Christians were accused of being Jewish and were tortured.

BENJAMIN: Well, I wouldn't have been caught!

MRS. SOLOMON: Perhaps not, but the Nazis thought of every trick to entrap the Jewish people.

ELLEN: Then why didn't the people rebel?

MRS. SOLOMON: You must remember that under the Nazi rule there were only Nazi newspapers and radio broadcasts. Of course, there was no television. The Jews were completely cut off from the outside world, except for rumors.

BENJAMIN: That's hard to imagine.

MRS. SOLOMON: People believed what they wished to believe. Everyone hoped and prayed for the war to end. And, when the United States joined the Allies against the Nazis, the people in the ghettos believed the war would be over in a matter of weeks, if not days.

MARK: But later many people did rebel, didn't they?

RUTH: That's right. You remember the documentary film our class saw on the uprising in the Warsaw ghetto.

MRS. SOLOMON: Yes. And there were rebellions in a number of other ghettos, too. But the war continued.

ELLEN: Thank God the Nazis were finally stopped!

ALAN: But not in time to save six million Jews.

BENJAMIN: Suppose a person refused to leave his home when the Nazis came. What would happen to him?

MRS. SOLOMON: Let me tell you a true story that took place in 1941 in a small city in Poland, two years after the Nazis invaded that country.

CURTAIN

Act II

TIME: *1941*

SETTING: *Plock, Poland*

AT RISE: MRS. SOLOMON *and the students stand at the left rear of the stage with their backs to the audience. They remain still all through Scene 2. Symbolically, these students and their teacher represent the people of the world who stood by in silence. A sign,* THE WORLD IS SILENT, *is visible.*

At the front of the stage, MRS. GOLDBERG *is lying sick in bed. Her husband is applying a cold compress to her forehead.*

MR. GOLDBERG: You still feel very warm. I wish we had a thermometer to take your temperature.

MRS. GOLDBERG *(In a quiet reassuring voice):* I will be all right, Abe. Just give me a little time.

MR. GOLDBERG: I wish Joseph hadn't been so careless and broken the thermometer.

MRS. GOLDBERG: Accidents happen. Besides, you can't expect everything to last forever.

MR. GOLDBERG: Who knows when we will be able to replace it?

MRS. GOLDBERG: Have patience, dear. The war will be over soon! It can't go on much longer.

MR. GOLDBERG *(Pacing the room impatiently):* I don't know! We have been hoping and praying for two years for this tyranny to be over. And still, there is no end in sight.

MRS. GOLDBERG: Hush. Don't let the children hear you speak like that. You will frighten them to death.

*(*MIRIAM *runs into the bedroom.)*

37

MIRIAM *(Frantic):* Papa, papa!

MR. GOLDBERG: Quiet, Miriam, you know your Mama is ill!

MIRIAM *(Out of breath):* Papa, the Nazis arrested Moshe, Itzhak, and three of their friends.

MR. GOLDBERG *(Placing his hand on Miriam's shoulder):* Did anyone say where they have taken them?

MIRIAM: No, Papa, no one knows. And there is a rumor that all of us will be deported to the East...to some cold, swampy region. We will have to clear the land...if we don't freeze to death.

MRS. GOLDBERG: Everyday there is another rumor.

MIRIAM *(Bending over her mother):* Mama, it's so cold there, and so wet. How are we going to live?

MRS. GOLDBERG *(Stroking Miriam's hair):* Now, Miriam, you said yourself it's just a rumor. Right?

MIRIAM: Yes, Mama.

MRS. GOLDBERG: How many rumors have we heard before? And we're still here, aren't we?

MIRIAM: But, Mama...

MR. GOLDBERG *(Interrupting):* Miriam, Mama is sick. Don't tire her now. Get ready for bed. We will talk about it tomorrow.

MIRIAM *(Protesting):* But, Papa...

JOSEPH *(Enters and walks toward his family with his head bowed.):* Hi, everybody.

MR. GOLDBERG *(Rushing toward JOSEPH):* Thank God you are home, Joseph. Did you hear about Itzhak and Moshe?

JOSEPH: Yes, Papa. I met Sophie on the way home from work. Her aunt and uncle are in a terrible state. Their only son, Pinchas, was taken away, also.

MR. GOLDBERG: Do they know where the Nazis took them?

JOSEPH: No, Papa. No one knows.

MIRIAM *(Tearfully):* When will this end, Papa? I am so afraid.

(MR. GOLDBERG hugs MIRIAM, but remains quiet.)

MRS. GOLDBERG *(In a weak voice):* Joseph, did you finish packing your knapsack?

JOSEPH: Yes, Mama.

MRS. GOLDBERG: Did you pack your warm pajamas?

JOSEPH: No, Mama, I didn't.

MRS. GOLDBERG: But Joseph, we must be prepared for anything.

(JOSEPH picks up his knapsack and brings it over to his mother.)

JOSEPH: It's full, Mama. There's no room left for another thing. My whole life's belongings are right here. I didn't know what to put in first.

MIRIAM: I do hope we will never have to leave this place with just a knapsack.

MR. GOLDBERG: Stop worrying. We are staying right here. *(Turning to his wife)* Can I get you anything before we go to sleep?

(THREE NAZIS with rifles in their hands, ready to shoot, approach the stage. One of them bangs on the door of the Goldberg apartment.)

FIRST NAZI: Raus, Juden, Raus!

SECOND NAZI: Out, Jews, out!

(*All* THREE NAZIS *break into the Goldberg apartment. The* GOLDBERGS *are terrified and huddle together in front of* MRS. GOLDBERG'S *bed, protecting the sick lady.*)

THIRD NAZI: You must report to the courtyard. You have five minutes to get ready. Five minutes, no more!

(*The other* TWO NAZIS *are searching the place, looking into every nook and cranny; poking with their guns. The Nazis leave the Goldberg's apartment, shouting and banging on other doors. Nazi voices are heard: "Out Jews, out!" The Nazis leave the stage.* MIRIAM *hugs her mother and sobs quietly.*)

MR. GOLDBERG (*Gently helping* MIRIAM *off of the bed*): Come now, Miriam, we must believe everything will turn out for the best. Help us get Mama dressed.

(MIRIAM *gets up slowly, and continues to sob.* JOSEPH *places his mother's shoes in front of the bed.* MIRIAM *removes the dress and sweater from the chair and puts them down on the bed. She proceeds to pull out coats and hats, lining them up on the chair.*
MR. GOLDBERG *and* JOSEPH *attempt to raise* MRS. GOLDBERG, *placing her feet over the side of the bed and helping her into a sitting position. While* MR. GOLDBERG *holds up his wife,* JOSEPH *and* MIRIAM *try to put on her socks and shoes.*
Suddenly, MRS. GOLDBERG *falls back.*)

MRS. GOLDBERG: It's no use, Abe, I can't go with you.

MR. GOLDBERG (*Encouraging his wife*): Now, now, Hannah. Of course you are coming with us. You must try to get dressed.

MRS. GOLDBERG: But I can't. Honest, I just can't.

MIRIAM (*Pleading*): Please, Mama, try for our sake. You must get dressed. We will help you; please try.

40

JOSEPH: Mama, you know we won't leave without you. And you know the consequences if we don't show up in the courtyard.

MRS. GOLDBERG: Abe, please. Please take the children and go.

(Again MR. GOLDBERG *lifts his wife into a sitting position.* MIRIAM *slips the dress on* MRS. GOLDBERG, *over her nightgown.* JOSEPH *holds up the sweater.)*

MR. GOLDBERG: Hannah, I wish you could stay in bed. God knows you need the rest. But we must get you up now. You will see, everything will be all right.

*(*MIRIAM *and* JOSEPH *help their mother with the sweater.* MR. GOLDBERG *lifts her coat from the chair. With the aid of* MR. GOLDBERG *and* JOSEPH, MRS. GOLDBERG *slowly stands up, but immediately falls back on the bed.)*

MRS. GOLDBERG: I can't walk. I can't even stand up with your help. The whole room is swaying back and forth. If it doesn't stop, I will pass out.

(The faces of MR. GOLDBERG, JOSEPH *and* MIRIAM *reflect fright and despair.)*

MR. GOLDBERG *(Attempting to be calm):* All right, Hannah, rest for a minute.

(He paces the room back and forth. JOSEPH *and* MIRIAM *follow him to the side of the room, where all stop.)*

MR. GOLDBERG *(Quietly but emphatically):* Joseph, you and Miriam fetch your coats and knapsacks! Go on down to the courtyard. I will stay here with Mama.

JOSEPH *and* MIRIAM: No, Papa, we are not leaving without you and Mama.

MR. GOLDBERG: But you must leave! The Nazis...

JOSEPH *and* MIRIAM *(Interrupting and sitting down):* No, Papa, we are staying right here with you and Mama.

MR. GOLDBERG (Raising his head and arms): Oh, God! What shall I do? What can I do? Please, help us!

(NAZI SOLDIERS, with rifles in ready position to shoot, line up on front left side of the stage, the courtyard. The yelling and banging of other Nazis is heard in the background: "Out, Jews, out! Make it fast! Hurry up!"

A few Jewish people, GHETTO RESIDENTS, carrying suitcases or knapsacks, assemble in front of the waiting Nazis. Other Nazi soldiers, machine guns in ready position, follow their victims and surround them.

A NAZI COMMANDER, his hands in his pockets, and an angry, impatient look about him, enters the stage and approaches a Nazi soldier.)

COMMANDER: Are they all here?

NAZI SOLDIER: We are proceeding with our last check, Herr Commandant.

The same THREE NAZI SOLDIERS, with machine guns and rifles, enter the Goldberg apartment.

FIRST NAZI (Angry and shouting): Why are you still here?

SECOND NAZI (Hitting MR. GOLDBERG with his rifle): Why aren't you in the courtyard?

THIRD NAZI: Didn't you understand our order?

(MR. GOLDBERG protects his head with his arms. MIRIAM and JOSEPH huddle closely together in front of their mother's bed. The FIRST NAZI pushes MIRIAM and JOSEPH away and looks down on MRS. GOLDBERG.)

FIRST NAZI: What do we have here?

MR. GOLDBERG (Rushing toward FIRST NAZI): Please, sir, my wife is ill. May we remain here with her?

JOSEPH: Please sir, let us stay. My father and I work in your uniform shop. Please let us stay here.

FIRST NAZI: No! No one remains in the ghetto.

SECOND NAZI: Get out to the courtyard before I shoot you down, everyone of you.

MRS. GOLDBERG: Joseph, Miriam, take your father, your coats and knapsacks and go ahead. I will be all right. May God be with you.

MIRIAM: No, Mama, no!

FIRST NAZI *(Poking* MIRIAM *with his rifle):* Go on. She is right.

*(*MIRIAM *and* JOSEPH *sit down on the floor and don't move. The* SECOND SOLDIER *places his rifle on Joseph's head. The* THIRD SOLDIER *aims his rifle directly at* MRS. GOLDBERG.*)*

THIRD NAZI: You three leave right this minute, or I shoot her now.

*(*JOSEPH *and* MIRIAM *run to their mother in an attempt to protect her.)*

THIRD NAZI *(Turning to* MR. GOLDBERG*):* Do you want to watch me kill all three of them?

MR. GOLDBERG *(Dazed and in shock, pulls on* MIRIAM'S *arm):* Come, Miriam. You, too, Joseph. *(They pick up their coats and knapsacks.)*

(Two of the NAZI SOLDIERS *follow the* GOLDBERGS, *poking their guns and pushing them out of the apartment, leaving* MRS. GOLDBERG *and* ONE NAZI *behind. In the courtyard they join the people, surrounded by Nazis. The captives, frightened and bewildered, quietly march off the stage, while the Nazis are shouting: "Schnell, move on! Hurry up! Hurry!")*

(After the captives and the Nazis leave the stage, all voices cease. The THIRD NAZI *guard aims his gun directly at* MRS. GOLDBERG'S *head and pulls the trigger. As the curtain falls, a gun shot is heard.)*

CURTAIN

PRODUCTION NOTES

SHADOWS OF THE HOLOCAUST-
NOW AND THEN

CHARACTERS: Scene 1: 6 male; 5 female. Scene 2: 6 male; 2 female; male extras for Nazi soldiers; male and female extras for ghetto Jews. (If not enough students are available for all parts, some of the characters in Act I may take the roles in Act II.)

PLAYING TIME: 20 minutes.

COSTUMES: Scene 1: Modern school clothing. Scene 2: Ghetto Jews wear 1940's street clothing with yellow stars attached to the left side of the chest. Mrs. Goldberg wears a nightgown. Nazis wear army uniforms with hats or helmets and boots. Red armbands with black swastikas on white circles are are worn on their left arms.

PROPERTIES: Bookbags, schoolbooks, and notebooks; U.S. and Czech birth certificates* (to be used with an overhead projector or reproduced on large posters); briefcase; large poster with the words THE WORLD IS SILENT; bed; chair; dress; sweater; pair of socks; small table; book; candle in candlestick holder; four knapsacks; suitcases; washcloths; rifles and guns.

SETTING: Scene 1: A school parking lot set in the present. Scene 2: The bedroom of an apartment in a Polish ghetto. A bed is located on the left side of the stage; a chair is to the right of the bed; a dress and sweater are hung over the chair, while shoes and socks are placed underneath it; a small table is to the right of the stage; a book and a lit candle are on the table; four knapsacks are lined up against the wall.

LIGHTING: Lights are dimmed for Act II.

SOUND: School bell and car horn as indicated in text.

---

*A copy of a Czech birth certificate is included in this resource book.

THE LETTER

In memory of my father, my sisters, my grandparents, and the rest of my family, who perished in the Holocaust.

THE LETTER

A Two-Act Play

CHARACTERS: ANA HEYMAN, BRENDA, CASTLE ATTENDANT, GHETTO PEOPLE, LEON, LISA, NARRATOR, PETER, RABBI HEYMAN, NAZI SS OFFICERS, RABBI POTASH, MR. WEISS

SETTING: ACT I : *The Ghetto of Riga, Latvia*
              ACT II: *Frankfort, Germany*

TIME: ACT I : *December 8, 1941*
              ACT II: *March, 1946*

Act I

Scene 1

SETTING: *A home in the Riga Ghetto*
TIME: *December 8, 1941*
AT RISE: LEON *enters the stage.* PETER *follows slowly behind him. Both boys appear sad and lost in their thoughts.*

LEON: Come on, Peter, hurry up! You still have some packing to do.

PETER: No, I don't. There is no more room in my knapsack.

LEON: Did you pack everything you want to take?

PETER: Are you kidding? I packed nothing I want to take!

LEON *(Puzzled):* Nothing?

PETER: Right, nothing.

LEON: Then you haven't packed.

PETER: Oh yes, I did.

LEON: Why didn't you pack the things you want?

PETER *(Frustrated):* Why? Why? You ask such silly questions! Wait till you start packing.

LEON: Well, what did you want to take?

PETER: Let's see. I wanted some of my books, but Dad said they were too heavy to carry.

LEON: Couldn't you take at least your favorite ones?

PETER: No, I couldn't. I wanted to take my skates, but Mom insisted I take a sweater instead.

LEON: They do say the climate is very cold in the East, where the Nazis plan to resettle us.

PETER: That's what they say. But I wanted to take my butterfly collection. You know, the one I started that summer we spent on the lake. But Mom said that I need warm pajamas. How much can you stuff into one knapsack anyway? The darn towels took up most of the space.

LEON: Gee, Peter, I see what you mean. I guess I'll have the same problem. I do hope I can take my stamp collection.

PETER: As bad as it is in this dreadful ghetto, I still wish they would leave us here until the end of the war.

LEON: But maybe life will be better in the new place. I can't imagine it being any worse!

PETER: I don't know, Leon. I don't trust Nazis or their promises.

LEON: I wish we didn't have to leave, either. But since we do, let's hope it will be better.

PETER: I guess you're right. You'd better hurry. We don't have much time.

LEON: Stop worrying, Peter. Let's see, today is December 8, 1941. I bet a year from now we'll be back in our own homes. The war can't last another year.

You'll see; we'll be OK.

(The boys leave the stage.)

SS OFFICERS: Schnell! Auf dem Platz! Quickly! Quickly! To the yard.

SS OFFICERS *(Yelling at the top of their voices):* Raus, Juden, Raus! Out, you Jews, out to the main yard!

(LEON, PETER, and other GHETTO PEOPLE, carrying suitcases and knap-sacks, are escorted off the stage by armed NAZI GUARDS.)

CURTAIN

Scene 2

SETTING: *The Heyman household*
TIME: *Later that day*
AT RISE: NARRATOR *is alone on stage.*
             To one side, ANA is packing a knapsack with clothing. Additional clothes, toiletries, and books are stacked nearby. ANA is frustrated, for nothing else will fit into her knapsack.

NARRATOR: In another part of the Riga Ghetto, in the house of the once prominent Heyman family, we find their youngest daughter, Ana.

ANA *(Frustrated):* How I hate to leave this home!

(ANA attempts to close the knapsack but fails, because it is too full. She removes some of the articles. While closing the bag and placing it on the floor, ANA speaks to the audience.)

ANA: Life in this ghetto brings a great deal of pain
     Each day is a struggle in every way.
     I wake in the morning, after a tortuous night,
     To sunshine that can't melt the gloom in my heart.

There must be a place, somewhere in this world,
Where children are laughing, and feeling secure,
No hunger pains, no fear of tomorrow,
No sadness around them, no more sorrow.

But I fear that the place we must go to now
Is not yet the one where we shall find freedom.
Rumors of danger keep my spirits low. Dear God,
I wish I could stay in my home 'til the end of the war.

(ANA *lifts a Bible from the table and clutches it to her chest. She paces the floor of her room. She stops abruptly and leafs through the Bible.)*

ANA: My father was so proud of this Bible. It was given to him by his grandfather! I wish I could hide it for my brother in America.

(ANA *looks around the room, searching for a hiding place. Suddenly, she stops.)*

ANA *(Full of hope and encouragement):* I know, I will write a letter and put it in the Bible. Perhaps someone will find the book and be kind enough to mail it to David.

(ANA *places the book on the table and picks up a pen and a sheet of paper. She sits down at the table to write the letter.)*

ANA *(Reading aloud as she writes):*

December 8, 1941

To Whom It May Concern:
  If you find this book, which has been in our family for many generations, please forward it to my brother, Rabbi David Heyman, in Philadelphia, U.S.A.
  The Nazis are next door. I don't know what will happen to me. Please remember us! And don't ever forget the murderers!
  May Justice triumph and be victorious forever!!!
            Thank you very much.
            Sincerely yours,
            Ana Heyman

(ANA *lifts the old volume and places her letter inside. She hears the sounds of marching guards. Quickly she places the book on the table and lifts her knapsack. At that moment two armed* NAZI GUARDS *bang on her door.)*

(*Outside her house,* ANA *and other* GHETTO PEOPLE *are escorted off the stage by the* NAZI GUARDS.)

CURTAIN

Act II

Scene 1

SETTING: *A street in Frankfurt, Germany.*
TIME: *March, 1946*
AT RISE: NARRATOR *is alone on stage.*

NARRATOR: The final defeat and total collapse of the Nazi regime came on May 9, 1945. By then, over 11 million innocent civilians, six million of them Jews, were brutally murdered. Now, almost a year later, here in Frankfurt, people still live in the shadow of the vast destruction. Alone and homeless, survivors, having searched in vain for family and friends, are overjoyed to meet anyone from their past.

(*The* NARRATOR *leaves the stage.* LISA *and* BRENDA *enter from opposite directions. They run toward each other and embrace.)*

BRENDA: Lisa! I am so glad to find you. Until yesterday, I had no idea that you were alive and living here in Frankfurt.

LISA: It was a lucky break meeting Joe. He told me you were here. I searched for my family, but no one survived.

BRENDA: I'm so sorry. It's hard to believe. You family was so big.

LISA: Every time I hear children play, or see them walking in the street, I turn to them in the hope that maybe it's my little brother or sisters. Even though I was told they all died in Poland, I still can't accept it.

BRENDA: I do the same thing. A few days ago, I saw a man walking on the sidewalk. From the back he looked just like my father. I ran after him, calling: "Daddy, Daddy." When the man turned around, I was disappointed and so embarrassed. The man must have thought I was a lunatic.

LISA: I'm sure he understood.

BRENDA: The Joint Distribution Committee is trying to locate my relatives in the United States. I don't remember their address.

(RABBI POTASH *and* RABBI HEYMAN *enter the stage. They walk toward the girls.)*

RABBI POTASH: Excuse us, ladies, would you know where the Joint Distribution Committee offices are?

BRENDA: Yes. Turn right at the next corner, and walk about a block. You will see the sign in front of the building on your left.

RABBI POTASH: Thank you very much.

(The RABBIS *leave the stage.)*

LISA *(Turning to her friend):* Brenda, I look at you, but I still can't believe that we are finally together. You are the only friend I've found from our home town. I can't tell you how happy I am to see you.

BRENDA: What are your plans? Will you be staying here long? Do you plan to go to Palestine or to join your relatives in America?

LISA: I really don't know yet what I will do. Can you come to my place, so we can talk for awhile?

BRENDA: Sure, I'd love to.

*(*LISA *and* BRENDA *leave the stage.)*

CURTAIN

Scene 2

SETTING: *The Joint Distribution Committee Office, Frankfurt, Germany.*

TIME: *Later that day.*

AT RISE: *Sam Weiss is seated behind a desk, reading a form, when a knock is heard.*

(RABBI POTASH *enters the office.* RABBI HEYMAN *follows behind him.* MR. WEISS *stands up.)*

RABBI POTASH *(Extending his hand to* MR. WEISS*)*: Good morning, Mr. Weiss; I'm Rabbi Sam Potash from New York City and this is my colleague, Rabbi David Heyman from Philadelphia.

MR. WEISS *(shaking hands with both men)*: Good morning. I am happy to meet you. You're a long way from home.

RABBI HEYMAN: Yes, we are. We didn't expect it would be so cold here at this time.

RABBI POTASH: So much snow for the end of March.

MR. WEISS: Yes, I must admit, the climate here in Frankfurt is rather cold. Now, what can I do for you, gentlemen?

RABBI POTASH: Mr. Weiss, we have learned that in a small town, around 100 kilometers from here, the Nazis collected thousands of Jewish books in an old castle.

MR. WEISS: What do you mean? The Nazis are known for having burned Jewish books, not for saving them.

RABBI HEYMAN: Let me explain. The Nazis confiscated Jewish books in the many communities the Germans occupied during World War II.

MR. WEISS *(Puzzled)*: That's incredible! Why would the Nazi murderers save Jewish books?

RABBI POTASH: These books were to serve as a reminder of the Nazi victory in the total destruction of European Jewry.

RABBI HEYMAN: Also, they were to be proof that large Jewish communities did exist before the Nazis ruled the world.

MR. WEISS (Shaking his head): I can't believe it!

RABBI POTASH: It's true. And we've come to ask if you would be kind enough to take us to that castle where the books are stored.

MR. WEISS: Yes, of course. I'd like to see that castle myself.

RABBI HEYMAN: We would like to go as soon as possible.

MR. WEISS: Let me see (Looking at his calendar) I am free tomorrow. I'll borrow a jeep from my friend. We shouldn't have too much trouble getting there.

RABBI POTASH: Thank you, Mr. Weiss. We do appreciate your help.

RABBI HEYMAN: From all we've heard about you, we knew we could count on your kindness. God bless you!

MR. WEISS: Believe me, I am just as anxious as you are to see those books. Meet me here tomorrow morning at 9 o'clock.

RABBI POTASH: Yes, of course.

RABBI HEYMAN: Thank you, Mr. Weiss. Until tomorrow then.

RABBI POTASH (Shaking hands with MR. WEISS): Shalom, Mr. Weiss.

MR. WEISS: Shalom!

(The RABBIS leave)

CURTAIN

Scene 3

SETTING: *A castle outside of Frankfurt, Germany*
TIME: *The next morning*
AT RISE: *Mr. Weiss and the two rabbis outside the castle*

RABBI HEYMAN *(Turning to* MR. WEISS*):* I thought we would never get here. Where did you learn to drive so well on snow in these treacherous mountains?

MR. WEISS: I'm used to driving in all kinds of weather.

RABBI POTASH: We are very fortunate to have you with us, Mr. Weiss. The countryside here is beautiful, and so is the castle.

RABBI HEYMAN: You're right.

MR. WEISS: Doesn't this view remind you of a winter scene on a picture post-card?

RABBI POTASH: It certainly does.

RABBI HEYMAN: What an irony! Books that were seized with such violence and terror are housed in complete peace and tranquility.

> *(Hesitantly,* MR. WEISS *pulls on the castle door bell. The* CASTLE ATTENDANT *opens the door.)*

CASTLE ATTENDANT: I've been expecting you. Please come in. The books are all in here. As you can see, many have not yet been unpacked.

> *(The men separate and walk to different shelves. They begin to leaf through the volumes.)*

RABBI POTASH *(Lifting a heavy book):* What a beautiful Chumash! It's from the city of Lodz in Poland.

> *(*RABBI HEYMAN *and* MR. WEISS *are preoccupied with the books on other shelves, each man absorbed in his task. Suddenly,* RABBI HEYMAN *screams out.)*

RABBI HEYMAN: Oh, my God! *(He falls to the floor, unconscious, clutching a book to his chest.)*

(MR. WEISS, RABBI POTASH, and the CASTLE ATTENDANT rush toward RABBI HEYMAN. RABBI POTASH bends over his friend and loosens his tie and shirt. MR. WEISS takes the book out of RABBI HEYMAN'S hand and puts it down on a carton. He checks the RABBI'S pulse.)

MR. WEISS *(Turning to the CASTLE ATTENDANT)*: Do you have a glass of water?

CASTLE ATTENDANT: Yes, just a moment.

(The CASTLE ATTENDANT leaves and returns quickly, handing the water to MR. WEISS. RABBI HEYMAN awakens slowly and sips the water. He looks confused.)

RABBI HEYMAN: What happened?

RABBI POTASH: You fainted.

RABBI HEYMAN: The book, where is my book?

MR. WEISS *(Picking up the book and returning it to him)*: You mean this book?

(RABBI HEYMAN pulls out a note from the book and hands it to MR. WEISS.)

RABBI HEYMAN: Please read this letter. It's from my sister, Ana, of blessed memory.

(MR. WEISS takes the letter from RABBI HEYMAN, while RABBI POTASH comes closer. Both men read the letter quietly.)

MR. WEISS *(Turning to RABBI HEYMAN in disbelief)*: Are you sure this letter is from your sister?

RABBI HEYMAN: I am positive! I'd recognize her handwriting anywhere. After I came to the States, Ana wrote to me often. And this is the Bible that belonged to my grandfather...and to his grandfather before him.

RABBI POTASH: What a brave girl your sister must have been.

RABBI HEYMAN: Yes, she was. One could always rely on Ana.

(MR. WEISS *comes to center front of the stage. He faces the audience and reads aloud Ana's letter.*)

MR. WEISS: *December 8, 1941*

To Whom It May Concern,
In case you find this book, which has been in our family for many generations, please forward it to my brother, Rabbi David Heyman in Philadelphia, U.S.A.
The Nazis are next door. I don't know what will happen to me. Please remember us! But don't ever forget the murderers!
May Justice triumph and be victorious forever!!!
Thank you very much,
Sincerely yours,
Ana Heyman

CURTAIN

PRODUCTION NOTES

THE LETTER

CHARACTERS: 6 male, 3 female; Narrator; 6 or more male and female extras for Ghetto People; 2 or more male extras for Nazi Guards.

PLAYING TIME: 15 minutes.

COSTUMES:

Act I: Ghetto Jews wear 1940's style street clothes with a yellow star attached to the left side of the chest. Nazi guards wear army uniforms with hats or helmets and boots; red armbands with black swastikas on white circles are worn on their left arms.

Act II: Lisa wears a blouse and skirt. Brenda wears a dress and hat. The rabbis wear dark suits, white shirts, ties and black hamburg hats. Mr. Weiss wears dark slacks and a white shirt with no tie. In Scene II, the Rabbis also wear top coats, hats and gloves. Mr. Weiss wears a winter jacket, gloves, and cap. The castle attendant wears a dark suit, white shirt, and bowtie.

PROPERTIES:

Act I: Knapsacks and/or suitcases for Leon, Peter, Ghetto People, and Ana; table and chairs; extra clothing and toiletries; books; an old Bible; writing paper; pencil; a kerosene lamp or lit candle; rifles.

Act II: A sign reading JOINT DISTRI-BUTION COMMITTEE; a desk with papers, books, and a telephone; a map of Europe; a chair; a castle door bell; bookcases filled with books, the old Bible; large cartons each bearing the name of a European city in bold black letters (Riga, Warsaw, Lublin, Krakow, Prague); a glass of water, Ana's letter.

SETTING:

Act I, Scene 1: A street in the Riga Ghetto. Backdrop shows rows of houses, small buildings, trees, and snow-covered streets. Scene 2: Ana's sparsely furnished living room with a table and two chairs in the center. Several books, an old Bible, writing paper, a pencil, and a kerosene lamp or lit candle are on the table. Extra clothing and toiletries are on the floor and chairs. A knapsack overflowing with clothing and possessions is on the floor.

Act II, Scene 1: A street in Frankfurt, Germany, March 1946. Backdrop shows 5-story buildings, some still with rubble from the bombing; street lights; and a kiosk. Scene 2: A small office. A sign, JOINT DISTRIBUTION COMMITTEE, is attached to the door. A desk with papers, books, and a telephone is down center. A map of Europe is on the wall. A chair is behind the desk. Scene 3: A room in a castle. A bell hangs on the door. The room is lined with shelves filled with books. Cartons marked with names of European cities are down center.

LIGHTING: Ana's room and the castle are dimly lit.

SOUND: The knocking on the office door and the ringing of the castle bell, as indicated in the text.

THE ESCAPE

To my mother, Brenda Rubinstein,
whose strength and courage gave me the
will to go on...

THE ESCAPE

A One-Act Play

CHARACTERS: NARRATOR, ESTHER, EVA, JUDITH, RACHEL, SARAH, CAMP PRISONERS, NAZI SOLDIERS

TIME: *January, 1943*

SETTING: *A concentration camp in Poland*

AT RISE: *Narrator alone on stage*

NARRATOR: *It is a very cold day in January, 1943. We are in a concentration camp in a thick forest in Poland. More than 50 young girls are housed in a wooden barrack here. It is getting dark. Some of the camp prisoners are returning to their barracks, after a long day of hard work in the ammunition factory. They are tired, sad, and very hungry.*

(ESTHER, EVA, JUDITH, RACHEL, *and* SARAH *walk slowly onto the stage, heads bowed. All sit down on stage floor, except* RACHEL. *She paces back and forth.)*

NARRATOR: The barrack is filled with tension and fear. A rumor is spreading quickly. Tomorrow the camp will be evacuated. Everyone has to leave. To where? No one knows.

(NARRATOR *walks off the stage.)*

JUDITH: Evacuated?

SARAH: Deported!

ESTHER: What does it mean?

EVA: Where will they take us?

JUDITH: How will we get there? Will we march in the snow? We have no boots!

ESTHER: Maybe by trucks? Or perhaps by train?

SARAH: You mean old, dirty cattle cars, don't you?

EVA *(Softly):* Will anyone make it?

RACHEL: Can't we hide?

SARAH: No, Rachel, we can't hide.

JUDITH *(Looking off somewhere):* Will I live?

(RACHEL *is pacing back and forth.)*

RACHEL *(Turning to Sarah):* Sarah, I've made a decision. I'm not going with the deportation.

SARAH *(Bewildered):* What do you mean?

RACHEL: I'm not leaving with you.

SARAH: What will you do?

RACHEL: I will hide here in the camp until everyone leaves.

JUDITH: But you will freeze or starve to death.

EVA: We have no food.

RACHEL: I know a non-Jewish family that may help me.

ESTHER: But how can they?

RACHEL: As soon as everyone leaves, I will escape from here and find my way to the Bilski family.

SARAH: That's impossible!

EVA: Where would you hide? Besides, look at your clothes and your face!

RUTH: Everyone can see that you come from the camp.

JUDITH: Do you know what you look like?

RACHEL: I guess so.

RUTH: I have an idea.

ALL THE GIRLS: What is it?

RUTH: Let's all give Rachel the best of everything we have, so she may have a chance to save herself.

(Silence. The girls look at one another, pacing back and forth.)

JUDITH *(Stopping abruptly):* What can I give her?

THE GIRLS *(Looking at* JUDITH*):* Let's see.

(The girls walk around JUDITH, *looking at her clothes.)*

EVA: Her clothes are too shabby.

JUDITH: I know. *(Turning to* RACHEL*)* Here, take my comb.

*(*JUDITH *hands the comb to* RACHEL.*)*

RACHEL: But Judith, it's the only thing you have.

JUDITH: I want you to have it! I wish I had more to give you.

RACHEL: Thank you, Judith.

SARAH *(Taking off her sweater):* Here, Rachel, take my sweater. My mother knitted it for me. It's held up really well.

RACHEL: Sarah, it's the only thing you have left from your mother.

SARAH: I know my mother would want you to have it. At least one of us will have a chance to survive.

ESTHER: My father made these ski slacks for me. He was a tailor, you know. I was arrested in late fall. That's why I have two pairs on. You can have one of them.

(ESTHER *takes off one pair of slacks, gives them to* RACHEL, *and sits on the floor.*)

RACHEL *(Almost in tears):* Girls, how can I ever thank you enough?

JUDITH: Live, Rachel, live! That will be the best way you can thank us.

EVA: There is another way to thank us.

RACHEL: What is it?

EVA: Live, Rachel, so that when the war is over, you can tell the world what life was like for us here in this death trap.

SARAH: Rachel, you'd better hurry. They will call us out for roll call any minute. You won't have time to hide.

RACHEL: I am not saying good-bye, I will say *lehitraot,* until I see you again!

(RACHEL *leaves the stage.*)

EVA: I wonder where Rachel will hide.

JUDITH: It's better we don't know her hiding place. Then they can't make us betray her, no matter how cruel their torture is.

ESTHER: I am scared they will find her. Every time anyone has tried to escape, she was caught and executed.

SARAH: Don't be so pessimistic. There is always a first time. Besides, Rachel knows these woods very well.

EVA: That's right. The camp is near her home town. Rachel told me that before the war, her family used to hike to this forest for picnics in the summer.

64

ESTHER: Just the same, I'm afraid for her. The Nazis will search every inch of this camp after they count us, and they'll discover one of us is missing.

SARAH: There's always a chance that Rachel will escape! I believe it. All of us must believe it.

EVA: At least one of us must survive. Please, God, let Rachel succeed! Let her be safe!

(A NAZI SOLDIER bangs on the barrack door with a whip.)

SOLDIER: Raus, Juden, Raus! Roll call! Come out, you Jews!

(The frightened girls glance at one another. Slowly, they walk out of the barrack. Other camp inmates join them. ESTHER remains sitting on the floor, her head resting in her cupped hands. SARAH comes toward ESTHER and gently tugs at her arm.)

SARAH *(Softly):* Come, Esther!

ESTHER: I want to go home!

SARAH: I know. All of us want to go home. But now we must report for roll call. Come! We can't be late!

(SARAH helps ESTHER get up from the floor, and together they walk out to join the other inmates, who have lined up for roll call. A NAZI SOLDIER, waving a whip, walks up and down in front of the inmates. Two NAZI SOLDIERS, with machine guns aimed at the prisoners, stand at each end of the line.)

SOLDIER: Attention! Start!

(The counting begins.)

FIRST PRISONER *(In line on the right):* ONE!

SECOND PRISONER: TWO!

THIRD PRISONER: THREE! *(and so on...)*

(Suddenly, there is the sound of running feet. The Nazis do not notice as RACHEL, *out of breath, joins the group from behind the line and moves up to* SARAH.*)*

RACHEL *(Whispering)*: I'm glad I made it in time!

SOLDIER: Achtung! Attention!

SARAH: What are you doing here, Rachel?

JUDITH: Why did you come back?

EVA: Rachel, we wanted so much for you to save yourself!

RACHEL: Quiet, girls, the guard will hear us. I had to come back!

ESTHER: Why, Rachel, why?

RACHEL: I was so busy worrying about myself and my hiding place, I forgot about you.

JUDITH: Us?

RACHEL: If the Nazis didn't find me, they would blame you for helping me. They would have killed all of you. Maybe I would have made it, but I could not have lived with myself knowing that all of you were killed so that I might live. Better that we stay together and hope, than you risk your lives just for me.

ESTHER: But at least one of us might have survived.

(The girls lower their heads and sadly turn away from RACHEL.*)*

RACHEL: Come on, girls. Don't be so gloomy. We must believe that all of us will live! Who knows, perhaps tomorrow the war will be over, or the next day. Don't lose hope! We must believe!

SARAH: Hope! That's the only thing we have.

(The girls begin singing "Ani Maamin," at first softly and then loud and clear. The cast joins in, and then the audience.)

CURTAIN

PRODUCTION NOTES

THE ESCAPE

CHARACTERS: 5 female; 2-4 male for Nazi soldiers; Narrator; male and female extras for camp inmates.

PLAYING TIME: 10 minutes.

COSTUMES: Inmates wear shabby street clothing. Each inmate wears a white patch (about 2x5 inches) on the left side of his chest. Each patch should have 4-5 different bold, black numerals printed on it. Sarah wears a sweater in good condition. Esther wears two pairs of slacks. Nazi soldiers wear army uniforms with hats or helmets and boots. Red armbands with black swastikas on white circles are worn on their left arms.

PROPERTIES: Comb; whip; rifles.

SETTING: A concentration camp in Poland in January 1943. Inside the barrack, the backdrop should show three tiers of shelves that served as beds; outside the barrack, the backdrop should have trees, other barracks, and watchtowers

LIGHTING: No special effects.

SOUND: Cast sings *Ani Maamin* or other appropriate song at end of play.

AT MY BAR MITZVAH—AND HIS

Dedicated to the memory of a thirteen-year-old hero of the Resistance.

Reader: When I was thirteen, I became Bar Mitzvah.
Assembly: *When he was thirteen, he became Bar Mitzvah.*

Reader: When I was thirteen, my teachers taught me—to put Tefillin on my arm.
Assembly: *When he was thirteen, his teachers taught him—to throw a hand grenade with his arm.*

Reader: When I was thirteen, I studied—the pathways of the Bible and roadways of the Talmud.
Assembly: *When he was thirteen, he studied—the canals of Warsaw and the sewers of the Ghetto.*

Reader: At my Bar Mitzvah, I took an oath to live as a Jew.
Assembly: *At his Bar Mitzvah, he took an oath to die as a Jew.*

Reader: At my Bar Mitzvah, I blessed God.
Assembly: *At his Bar Mitzvah, he questioned God.*

Reader: At my Bar Mitzvah, I lifted my voice and sang.
Assembly: *At his Bar Mitzvah, he lifted his fists and fought.*

Reader: At my Bar Mitzvah, I read from the Scroll of the Torah.
Assembly: *At his Bar Mitzvah, he wrote a Scroll of Fire.*

Reader: At my Bar Mitzvah, I wore a new Tallit over a new suit.
Assembly: *At his Bar Mitzvah, he wore a rifle and bullets over a suit of rags.*

Reader: At my Bar Mitzvah, I started my road of life.
Assembly: *At his Bar Mitzvah, he began his road to martyrdom.*

Reader: At my Bar Mitzvah, family and friends came—to say l'chayim.
Assembly: *At his Bar Mitzvah, Rabbi Akiba and Trumpeldor, Hannah and her seven sons came—to escort him to Heaven.*

Reader: At my Bar Mitzvah, they praised my voice, my song, my melody.
Assembly: *At his Bar Mitzvah, they praised his strength, his courage, his fearlessness.*

Reader: When I was thirteen, I was called up to the Torah—I went to the Bimah.
Assembly: *When he was thirteen, his body went up in smoke—his soul rose to God.*

Reader: When I was thirteen, I became Bar Mitzvah—and lived.
Assembly: *When he was thirteen, he became Bar Mitzvah—and lives now within each of us.*

A PRECIOUS GIFT

In memory of my parents and Erik

I was in Poland, and it was a time of war. For the Jews of Europe, it was a long and terrible war. It had been five years since my family was forced to leave our home in Czechoslovakia and begin a journey to an unknown, new life. No one imagined that the new life would be so very sad and cruel.

My father and I were in a concentration camp, a place nothing like our home. We were caged behind barbed-wire fences. Every day we were marched to work in ammunition factories, always watched from both sides by German guards. There was no escape for us. We lived in barracks, many women or men in the same huge room. Our beds were hard, wooden planks. And we were hungry. Always hungry.

It had been more than two years since I last saw my mother. She was taken away in a cattle train with many other Jews from our city. Their destination was unknown. We heard terrible rumors about what happened, but I just could not believe them. I refused to believe them. I thought about my mother every day, and I missed her. How I missed her!

My only brother, Erik, was shot over a year ago, when we were in a different concentration camp. They shot all the children under the age of 16. I was 13 at the time. I don't know how I survived. I can still hear the sound of the machine guns that killed him. How could Erik be dead? He was just 11 years old. It was the only time in my life that I wanted to die, but I had to live. I was all my father had left. I had to live for him.

My father worked the day shift, and I worked some days and some nights, yet we managed to see each other every day. We lived for our short, precious moments together.

One day, standing in line for food, I held a place for my father. The other prisoners did not mind, because I was one of the few children in the camp, and they protected me whenever they could. But this evening my father did not show up. I took my bowl of soup for him and went to his barrack. He was in bed. He said he was too tired to come to supper, but I knew this was not true. I later learned that earlier in the day he'd found a carrot in a trash can near the camp's kitchen and had taken it for me. He was caught and beaten terribly. He missed coming to the food line because he could not move. But he managed to hide his pain from me.

Outside the camp, life continued. Families were together and the seasons changed. For us, time had no meaning. Each day was the same. Fear, sadness, hunger, and hope dominated our lives.

It was winter again. In my other life, in my world back home, I looked forward to winter, because it brought my birthday. But here, in this place, what was the point of remembering. Most of us did not even know what day of the month it was. What difference would it make? And how could one celebrate a birthday? We had nothing to give.

Yet my father remembered. He must have thought about it for weeks ahead of time. When we met on December 22, his eyes were full of tears. He had a birthday gift for me. It was a simple, steel comb which he had made in the camp's workshop. I could not imagine how he'd done it, since German overseers watched us all the time to make sure prisoners were doing their jobs. What a terrible risk he had taken to make this gift for me. The comb was crude; its teeth were not completely even. But to me, it was the most beautiful gift.

From that day on, I carried the comb with me to work, and I kept it in my bed at night. It was always with me. Days passed, months passed, and still I treasured my comb.

One day, orders came to evacuate the camp. Once more, men and women were separated and hoarded into cattle trains. This time, we were shipped to a concentration camp in Germany. When we arrived, I found out that my father had been shipped elsewhere. I had no idea where. New horror and sadness came over me.

We were ordered to put all of our clothing and possessions in a pile. I had written a collection of poems and stories. It was hard for me to give them up, but I put them on the pile, too. But under no circumstances would I give away my precious comb. Hidden by a crowd of frightened women, I dug a hole in the ground and buried it. I thought that if I lived through the day, I would be able to find it again.

We were led to big rooms, where they shaved our heads and gave us striped, prisoners' clothes. When we came back out, I tried to remember where I had hidden my comb. I did not realize how difficult it would be. It had been so crowded, and I'd been so scared when I buried it. I looked a long time, but couldn't find the comb.

Many times during my stay in the camp, I tried to find my comb, always frightened the guards would catch and punish me. To my great sadness, I was never able to find it.

The war ended a very long time ago. Since then, I have received many gifts which have meant a lot to me. But still I am sad that I never found the gift, given to me with so much love, in a place where there was nothing to give.

ZOG NIT KEYNMOL

Words by Hirsh Glik

Zog nit keyn - mol az du geyst dem lets - tn

veg, Chotsh him - len blay - e - ne far - shte - ln bloy - e teg;

Ku - men vet noch und - zer oys - ge - benk - te sho, S'vet a

poyk ton und - zer trot: mir ze - nen do!

A song of hope sung by the Jewish partisans. "The hour for which we yearn will yet arrive, and our marching steps will thunder, 'We survive!'"

ANI MA'AMIN

Lento religioso

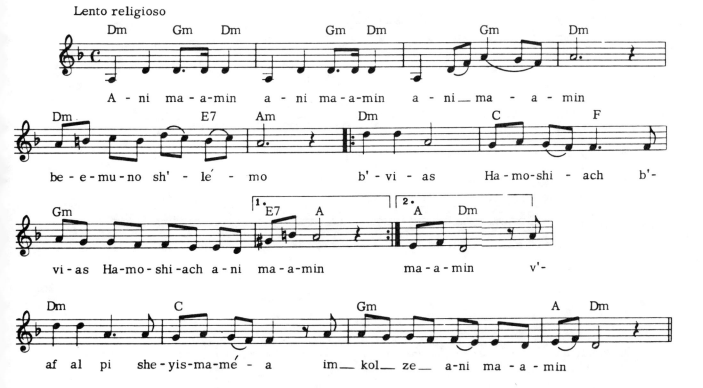

A - ni ma - a - min a - ni ma - a - min a - ni ma - a - min

be - e - mu - no sh' - le' - mo b' - vi - as Ha - mo - shi - ach b'-

vi - as Ha - mo - shi - ach a - ni ma - a - min ma - a - min v'-

af al pi she - yis - ma - mé - a im kol ze a - ni ma - a - min

I believe in the coming of the Messiah, and even if he delays, I will believe. The Jews of Europe sang this song as they marched to the gas chambers.

73

ROJINKES MIT MANDLEN

The lonely widow sings her child a lullaby about a little white goat who will bring a treat of raisins and almonds.

AM YISRAEL CHAI

Music by Rabbi Seymour Rockoff

The people of Israel live!

HATIKVAH

Words by Naftali Imber

Israel's national anthem.

Music courtesy of Velvel Pasternak

GLOSSARY

Appell—roll call. Camp prisoners had to assemble each morning and night to be counted. Appell was often accompanied by beatings and humiliation. If a prisoner was missing, his entire barrack might be punished or even killed.

Concentration camp—Camps created by the Nazis for Jews, gypsies, political enemies, prisoners of war, and others the Nazis thought to be "undesirable." The camps were surrounded by barbed wire, and armed guards supervised and often beat the inmates. Prisoners slept on wooden planks in crowded barracks and lived on a starvation diet. Some camps supplied forced labor for munitions factories, mines, and industry. When people became too sick to work, they were killed. Other camps were designed specifically for extermination. Jews were taken from transports directly to gas chambers. Once dead, their bodies were cremated.

Deportation—banishment. The Nazis forced the Jews to leave their cities and ghettos and be transported to labor and death camps.

Evacuation—the withdrawal of a population from a city. Jews were evacuated from hundreds of communities and moved to ghettos or deported to camps.

Ghetto—an Italian word which has come to mean the area of a city inhabited by Jews. During the Holocaust, Nazis forced a city's entire Jewish population into a small area surrounded by a wall. Jews could leave only with permission and generally only for forced labor. Eventually the ghettos were evacuated, and Jews were deported to concentration camps.

Holocaust—destruction of a whole people by fire. The name given to the destruction of two-thirds of Europe's entire Jewish population during World War II.

Joint Distribution Committee—the agency created to distribute overseas relief funds collected by American Jewish organizations. The "Joint" helped thousands of Jewish displaced persons rebuild their lives after the Holocaust, by providing food, clothing, job training, social workers, and medical personnel.

Liberation—setting free. As the Allied armies reconquered Europe from the Nazis, Jews were liberated from concentration camps and other forms of Nazi imprisonment.

Nazi—a member of the National Socialist Party, the anti-semitic political party headed by Adolf Hitler which came into power in Germany in 1933, and conquered the countries of Europe until defeated by the Allies in 1945. The Nazis systematically destroyed the Jewish populations of all countries it occupied.

Transport—the name given to the cattle trains which transported Jews to concentration camps. The trip usually lasted several days, and many died from the overcrowding, hunger, thirst, and disease.

HELPFUL HINTS FOR A MEANINGFUL
HOLOCAUST ASSEMBLY

PREPARATION

• Holocaust assemblies are most effective if the audience is prepared. Before the assembly, teachers should receive copies of the play and/or readings that will be presented, so they may review important concepts, vocabulary and historical material with students.

• In order to include original material in the assembly program, students should be encouraged to write poems, short essays, letters, and prayers reflecting their feelings. Teachers may choose a few to be presented at the assembly and others to print in the assembly program.

• Invite interested students to illustrate the assembly program cover and/or work on posters, murals, and scenery for the plays.

• Remember to list the names of all students and faculty whose efforts contributed to the program.

SETTING AND MOOD

• Students should be encouraged to view the Holocaust assembly as a memorial service and not as entertainment. Some teachers prefer to hold programs in a sanctuary rather than in an auditorium. Soft, somber background music helps to quiet an audience quickly. Request that there be no applause at the program.

THE PROGRAM

• Keep the program to a time limit appropriate to the audience. Encourage audience participation through songs and responsive readings. Check all material for vocabulary. Replace difficult words with simple, clear language where necessary.

ADAPTING THE PLAYS

• Production notes should be seen as guides. These plays may be done without scenery and with few props. Roles may be combined if fewer players are available.

• Some teachers object to students playing the roles of the oppressors. If so, we suggest students wear masks or that voice-overs be used instead of actors.

• If available, the overhead projector can be a useful dramatic tool. Use it to project the birth certificates mentioned in *Shadows of The Holocaust,* Ana's letter in *The Letter,* or to create scenery.

AFTERWARD

• It is helpful if children have a chance to discuss their feelings, questions, and even fears after a Holocaust program. Teachers also may wish to inform parents of the nature of the assembly so that families are prepared to discuss the program at home.

SUGGESTED FORMAT FOR A
HOLOCAUST MEMORIAL PROGRAM

Opening Remarks

Song*

Poems and Readings—original material or selections from Holocaust literature

Song

Play, Story, Film, or Lecture

Song

Memorial Candle Lighting**

Kaddish or *El Mole Rachamim*

Closing Song

*Several songs are included in this anthology. Some teachers begin assemblies with Hatikvah; others find it an appropriate closing song.
**May be done by survivors, their children or grandchildren.

BIBLIOGRAPHY

There are many outstanding bibliographies of Holocaust books and resources for young people. We recommend the following:

Altshuler, David and Lucy Dawidowicz. *Hitler's War Against the Jews.* New York: Behrman House, 1978.
Meltzer, Milton. *Never to Forget.* New York: Harper and Row, 1976.
Stadler, Bea. *The Holocaust.* New York: Behrman House, 1973.
"Teaching About the Holocaust." *The Pedagogic Reporter.* Jewish Education Service of North America, 114 Fifth Ave., NYC 10011, 1982.
Teaching the Holocaust—Resources and Materials. Social Studies School Service, 10,000 Culver Blvd., Culver City, CA 90230. 1983.

ABOUT THE AUTHORS

HARRIET STEINHORN was born in Lodz, Poland. When she was 10, her family was forced to move into the Skarzysko Ghetto in Poland. Three years later, she was separated from her family and sent to a forced labor camp. She spent the following three years in five concentration camps and was liberated from Bergen-Belsen on April 15, 1945. All of her immediate family, except for her mother, perished in the Holocaust.

After regaining her health in Sweden, Harriet came to the U.S. in 1949. She married and is the mother of three children. She received degrees in education and Hebrew literature and has been teaching in Silver Spring, Maryland for the past 18 years. She has created curricula for Holocaust studies; frequently lectures and presents workshops for area schools, churches, and synagogues; and has written extensively on the subject. Her play, *The Escape,* received a curriculum enrichment award from the Greater Washington Jewish Educators Assembly.

EDITH PICK LOWY was born in Czechoslovakia and is a survivor of six camps. She was liberated from a death march in Germany. After the war, she lived in Israel for 11 years and came to the U.S. in 1958, where she received her teacher training. Edith teaches Hebrew at the Jewish Day School in Rockville, Maryland. She is married and the mother of two daughters.